D0910451

HOMES
& GARDENS
LIBRARY OF
INTERIORS
Bedrooms

HOMES
& GARDENS
LIBRARY OF
INTERIORS
Bedrooms
Amanda Evans

PAVILION

To Beatrice, who so patiently waited until I had finished this text before being born

First published in Great Britain in 1997 by
Pavilion Books Ltd
26 Upper Ground
London SE1 9PD

Designed by Peter Bennett
Picture research by Kate Duffy

A CIP catalogue record for this book is available from the British Library.
ISBN: 1 85793 962 X

Typeset in Gill Sans Medium
Printed and bound in Spain by Bookprint

10 9 8 7 6 5 4 3 2 1

This book may be ordered by post direct from the publisher.
Please contact the Marketing Department.
But try your bookshop first.

Acknowledgements

The publisher would like to thank the following sources of providing the photographs for this book:
Robert Harding Picture Library/IPC Magazines 14 /**Jan Baldwin** 6 bottom, 9, 10 bottom, 12 centre, 15, 20 top, 26 top, 31 top, 33, 57, 58, 62 top, 63 centre, 64, 66 top, 70, 72 top, 77 bottom, 83 right, 91 right /**David Barrett** 27 centre, 78 bottom, 88 /**Tim Beddow** 6 centre, 22, 50 left /**Simon Brown** 8 centre, 10 centre, 24 bottom /**Peter Cook** 28 centre, 30 /**Christopher Drake** 11 centre, 13 top & centre, 18, 19, 21 left, 25, 29 bottom, 37 bottom, 41, 44 centre, 45 top, 46 bottom, 49, 50 right, 54, 55, 59, 75 top, 76 top, 78 centre, 86, 91 left /**Scott Hawkins** 8 bottom, 27 top, 34 /**Tom Leighton** 6 top, 13 bottom, 23 bottom, 24 top, 77 top, 82 /**Hannah Lewis** 76 bottom, 80 top /**Mark Luscombe-Whyte** 28 bottom, 36 bottom, 85 /**Nadia Mackenzie** 26 bottom, 32 bottom, 61 top, 66 bottom /**James Merrell** 7 top, 12 bottom, 21 right, 23 top, 29 centre, 40 top, 42 bottom, 44 bottom, 45 centre & bottom, 46 top, 48, 51, 52, 71 top /**David Montgomery** 60 top, 65 top /**David Parminter** 65 bottom /**Jonathan Pilkington** 16 bottom, 28 top, 36 top, 60 bottom, 61 bottom, 67, 69 /**Bill Reavell** 68 right /**Trevor Richards** 20 bottom, 32 top, 46 centre, 53, 62 centre, 72 bottom, 90 /**Paul Ryan** 7 bottom, 8 top, 44 top, 63 top & bottom, 73, 75 bottom, 78 top, 81, 87 bottom /**Simon Upton** 7 centre, 60 centre /**Fritz von der Schulenburg** 11 bottom, 17 left /**Andreas von Einsiedel** 10 top, 11 top, 12 top, 16 top, 17 right, 38, 39, 71 bottom /**Polly Wreford** 56, 80 bottom, 84.
Grange 31 bottom, 62 bottom, 74; **Heal & Son** 77 centre, 89; **The Holding Company** 61 centre; **Laura Ashley** 37 top, 42 top; **McFadden Cabinetmakers** 27 bottom, 35, 68 left; **The Pier** 29 top, 40 bottom; **Shaker** 26 centre, 43; **Simon Horn** 83 left, 87 top; **Vi-Spring** 76 centre.

Contents

Introduction

Probably the most personal space in the whole house, the bedroom is often where we are most self-indulgent in terms of fulfilling our wildest decorating dreams. Here, unlike other rooms in your home, there is no one else's taste or practical requirements to take into consideration. Your bedroom is a room for you and the person you share it with. This means you can be as extravagant, as idiosyncratic, as single-minded or as austere as you like with the look of this room.

In purely practical terms, the bedroom is a place for sleeping and dressing. But to restrict it to these activities alone is to underestimate its importance as a multi-faceted room. It is a private sanctuary: the place we tend to go when we want comfort, rest, peace or mollycoddling. And how we decorate the bedroom reflects what we want out of it. What could be nicer than a summer afternoon's siesta with a gentle breeze wafting the calico curtains?

Or curling up in the prettiest of armchairs on a rainy winter's day. Some of us use the peace of our bedrooms to write letters. Some read or sew. Others even exercise. Those with children may well see it as a refuge from noisy breakfasts or, alternatively, a place that can accommodate the whole family for early-morning tea. After a busy day at work, it may be the place to put your feet up and relax. It is also where you begin every day, and the quality of that beginning is surely dependent on the way in which you have decorated the room. The bedroom, therefore, is a private domain and should be as individual as the inhabitant.

Before choosing the decorating style ask yourself a few practical questions. For instance, what else other than sleeping and dressing will you use your bedroom for? Is there a window with a view you can take advantage of? Might you like a writing desk in here? Or a sofa? Is this where you will keep all your books, and if so do you want built-in shelves or free-standing bookcases?

Whatever decision that you come to about the additional functions of your bedroom it is at this point that you must pause to think about the lighting and any requirements you may have for sockets, wall lights or spotlights. Embark upon any re-wiring now, before serious decorating work begins. Remember, you cannot ever have too many electrical sockets in a room, but it is worth making a few major decisions now, such as where your bed, dressing table, writing desk or armchair might be placed, so that your sockets are strategically placed for lights, clocks, radios, etc., without revealing trailing wires.

Once the hardcore practicalities are sorted, you can turn your mind to the fun part. What is your bedroom to look like? Traditional or contemporary? Unashamedly feminine or strictly minimalist? Is it to be decorated with a pretty wallpaper or a historical paint colour?

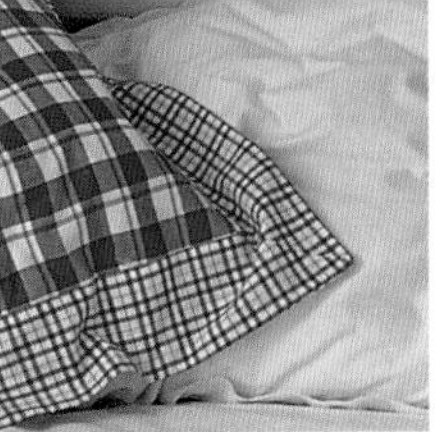

The basic ingredients will, of course, be your bed, and to a large extent the style of the bed will dictate the look of the room. But even a simple wooden bed can be dressed in a number of different ways to suit different styles.

Flooring will be another important consideration. Practicality is most people's priority: the majority of bedrooms tend to be carpeted because this offers warmth and comfort under bare feet. But there is no reason why you couldn't choose polished wooden floorboards for a very different effect, and create that same warmth underfoot with a scattering of rugs.

The soft furnishings are a project in themselves. Whatever curtain fabric you choose, don't forget to think about the effect they will have once hung at the window. Most fabrics will need some sort of inner lining at the very least to ensure that early-morning light does not stream in, but many people will want the addition of black-out material. A combination of blinds and curtains in the same fabric can also be effective in filtering out daylight and avoiding dawn awakenings in the summer.

The furniture you choose will, to a large extent, depend on the style of your bedroom. But most of us will require a few basic pieces: a bed, which could be any number of styles, from an elaborate four-poster to a simple Oriental futon; cupboards, either fitted or free-standing; bedside tables to contain successfully the paraphernalia that often builds up – books, tissues, light, clock, telephone, water glasses, for instance; and a chest of drawers or

perhaps a dressing table to store both clothes and the vast amounts of small items we all tend to hoard such as jewellery, make-up, hankies and hairbrushes. A blanket box is useful for storing spare bedding, and can double up as seating.

Turning your bedroom into a private haven takes much enjoyable research and thought. This book aims to give you endless inspiration – no matter what look you eventually choose. Within these pages you will find a wide range of bedroom styles, colours and ideas that together offer all the ingredients you need to select from in order to create your own individual bedroom.

Traditional

A traditional bedroom will conjure up wildly different images to different people. The one thing you can safely say, however, is that it will *not* be old fashioned. The traditional look draws from a wide range of historical periods and nationalities, but even 'tradition' moves on. Thus the conventional elements of a traditional bedroom – chintz, overblown flowers, antique wooden furniture and lacy white linen – will be constantly updated by designers and manufacturers to produce today's version of the traditional room.

Inspiration for creating a traditional bedroom is likely to come from a number of sources. The timeless elegance of the English country house is probably the most widely used starting point. The essential ingredients vary only in their degrees of grandness, but the very essence of this look will revolve around elegant chintz or linen curtains decorated in billowing country flowers such as honeysuckle or climbing geraniums. There will be a few pieces

of good wooden furniture – perhaps a simple tall-boy and bedside tables. A dressing table is likely to be placed in front of the window, and will either be a frothy, flounced affair using the same fabric as the curtains, or an unembellished wooden table with drawers and a wood-framed mirror. Silver and glass accessories will adorn the dressing table, as will ranks of ubiquitous family photographs. The generous bed is covered in an elegantly faded, flowery eiderdown or a knobbly cream throw. The walls will be papered in simple stripes or sprigged flowers, and the overall effect is effortless and relaxing.

Bedrooms

This approach is often taken to extremes in an urban environment, where the word traditional can occasionally mean nothing but unbridled chintz. But it doesn't have to this way; put together with skill it can be a marvellously exuberant elaboration of the country-house look. Here is your chance to make great use of historical window treatments, such as swags and tails, full pelmets and heavy fabric held open with large tasselled tie-backs. Huge, square pillows with delicate lacy covers will look inviting piled in abundance on the bed. Fabrics and wallpapers will co-ordinate, and there will be at least one matching upholstered armchair or sofa.

You are most likely to use interesting paint finishes on cupboards, doors and dado rails. The basic repertoire of ragging, scumbling and rolling has been supplemented by increasingly elaborate finishes, and it is always worth asking a specialist painter to show you sample boards and to try out small patches on your walls before embarking on a finish that is going to totally overpower the rest of the room.

Another strong influence for the traditional bedroom is the country cottage – a look that has its roots not just in England, but worldwide, particularly America. This simpler style is one that has become beloved of many interior decorators and designers over the last decade or so. As a result it is now all too easy to produce a cliché rather than a natural ambience. For there is nothing worse than a cheap-looking, modern version of a Victorian patchwork quilt, or a stiff arrangement of artificially bright dried flowers.

At its most spartan the traditional country-style bedroom consists of bare floorboards, a simple wooden bed, cotton bedspread, plain white walls and unfussy curtains: effortless, and tranquil.

At the other extreme is the glorious overflowing of all your most treasured possessions – heirloom samplers on the wall, a softly worn patchwork quilt, crisp lace and embroidered linen sheets and floral fabrics. You don't

have to live in a cottage or, indeed, the country to enjoy this style, as it can be very easily adapted for so many different interiors using variants of a few basic ingredients. The bed, for instance, could either boast an elaborate iron bedhead, or be a simple wooden design. The walls might be colour-washed in traditional colours of cream buttermilk, ochre or old pink which would suit the uneven plaster walls of a country property. On the other hand, wallpaper of the prettiest stripes or delicate rosebuds would be every bit as successful in creating a rural atmosphere in an urban property.

Occasionally, stencilling might be used, but it should be judicious and limited to simple designs, using subtle paint-tones that blend so well with the colour of the wall that they are only just discernible. Tongue-and-groove panelling on the wall produces an instant effect and looks just as good in a modern house as it does in the perfect

country cottage.

What you do with the floor in a traditional bedroom will depend entirely on what is already there. If the floorboards are in good condition they are worth polishing and exposing. Scatter with rugs, choosing either the mellow tones of antique kilims or the pastel shades of cotton dhurries. You could also think about a natural floor covering like sisal or seagrass, but remember this can be hard underfoot, so it is always a good idea to pop a few softer rugs down at strategic places, such as the side of the bed or in front of the wardrobe.

The curtains you choose will entirely depend upon the size and shape of your window, but generally speaking the design will be simple. Checks or stripes work well, as does plain calico. For a softly feminine look, an embroidered white tablecloth hung from a metal pole is extremely effective. Appropriate accessories will complete the look, and here is your chance to over-indulge without getting it wrong. Jugs filled with flowers from the garden,

lace panels at the windows, simply framed pictures massed on the walls, antique blanket chests or upholstered ottomans, grandmother's patchwork quilt, and all the old family photographs you can lay your hands on.

In between these two looks, the variety of traditional styles is endless. Your bed, for instance, could be anything from a curtained four-poster to a much simpler one with a padded bedhead. At the end of the bed you might place an old sofa covered with a pretty bedspread, or, perhaps, a desk. The cupboard you choose might well be an elegant free-standing wooden design or a wall of fitted units. If the latter is the case, remember that to fit in with a traditional look you will need to ensure that the doors are panelled – they may even have glass panels, hung behind with fabric. Any fabric or wallpaper in the room is likely to be patterned; accessories may well be antique. Make a habit of scouring junk shops and antique fairs for interesting accessories, such as silver hairbrushes or picture frames to complete the look you want.

As always, the thing to consider is what you want out of your bedroom and how this fits in with your chosen style. Writing desks, wooden sewing tables, sofas and open fires are all in keeping with the traditional look. High-tech metal exercise equipment is not.

Creating the look of a traditional bedroom does not depend on historical accuracy, but on the furniture and accessories you choose and how you put them together. Enjoy it, and the room you create will reflect that pleasure.

The owner of this bedroom has taken advantage of the beautiful views by placing her writing table in front of the elegant sash window. Shades of dove grey throughout give the room a calm serenity and thanks to the original wooden shutters it is possible to keep the look simple and clean. Little pattern is required in this room. It is texture that plays a major role: the layered, self-patterned bedspreads, and the glossed tongue-and-groove panels create a simple, traditional room.

Abundance is the key to this unashamedly feminine, cottage-style bedroom. Several different fabric designs are artfully held together, using blue and white as the common theme. This is not a big room, and the owner has decided to make a bold statement by filling most of it with the pretty four poster. An old sofa is covered with a quilted cotton bedspread and placed at the end of the bed, creating a sense of space that is deceptive. A lace tablecloth is flung over the bed frame.

Right: Wooden furniture does not have to be of the same period for the pieces to work well together in a room. Here the dark tones blend harmoniously, and are offset by the warm, honey-coloured walls. Below: This twin-bedded room shows how potentially sombre wooden furniture can be given a fresh, bright look with the introduction of blue and white. The room is pulled together by the matching, boldly patterned eiderdowns and unobtrusive coronas.

Right: The traditional bedroom relies on warmth, mellow tones and texture. Here a collection of silver and cut-glass accessories are simply displayed on the games table. The button-backed chair and embroidered cushion look comfortably inviting. Left: Natural fabrics and colours have been used in this room. A simple four-poster frame is softened by the addition of a muslin pelmet and curtains. Use of pattern is kept to a minimum with a crewel-work bedspread and pillows.

This is a contemporary interpretation of the traditional bedroom. Its sumptuous design positively explodes with pattern, yet, thanks to the simple colour scheme, it remains surprisingly calm. The big fabric design, an all-time favourite from Manuel Canovas, hangs from a corona by McKinney, turning the bed into a regal affair. The same fabric is used to cover the wall and is finished off with grosgrain ribbon. This is a marvellous trick if you don't want to replaster uneven walls.

This room takes its style from the original country-house look. Matching fabric for the curtains, bed drapes and eiderdown is generously used without being obtrusive. Plain, powder-blue walls are a perfect foil for the flowery chintz, and the yellow-and-white checked fabric inside the bed drapes helps to make this room seem less formal. The gothic arch carved at the top of the bookcase echoes the shape created by the Italian strung curtains.

Right: A monochromatic scheme such as this could so easily seem bleak. However, thanks to the addition of the crispest white bedlinen and a small posy of lilac flowers, the room takes on a chic simplicity of its own. The grey walls work perfectly with the black-and-white prints. Below: Working with a beamed ceiling need not hinder an exuberant style. This heavily draped four-poster sits square and tall in the room. The bold fabric is used in quantity and the effect is inviting.

Left: There can be no greater confidence than to mix, with such verve, old and new in this way. A brightly coloured modern print hangs against the strongly patterned traditional *toile de jouy*. A plump armchair is placed near the fireplace to give this bedroom its perfect reading corner. Right: A round, glass-topped table provides unusually capacious bedside storage and display. Wall sconces, table lamps and cosy reading lights give this room an indisputably feminine feel.

Bedrooms have to work visually for both male and female occupants. A good compromise is this combination of strong wood and minimal lace. Here, the simple frill with its fan-edged fringe leaves much of the bold wood to view. The antique barley-twist four-poster, gilt-framed mirror and old prints are given a surprisingly up-to-date feel by combining them in a minimal colour scheme. Shades of grey and white are extremely effective in creating a sense of space.

Top: A dressing table placed in front of a window is the perfect place to make up. This particular example, with its frilled pelmet and surround, is one of the essential ingredients of a traditional country-house bedroom. Two simple candlestick lamps link the different elements on display. Above: A good night's sleep is guaranteed with these angels watching over you. The Tattersall checks, stripes and fabric flowers, all from the same palette, give off a warm glow.

The all-embracing, slightly indulgent qualities of *toile de jouy* make it a perfect choice for a traditional bedroom. Using fabric to cover the walls is the perfect way to hide a multitude of sins underneath, and the result is unbelievably inviting. Right: The owners of this room have resisted the temptation to use this alcove as a fitted cupboard. Instead, it has become an ingeniously private sleeping area. A variety of different fabrics, paint and wallpaper all have Suffolk as the theme.

The end of the bed is often surprisingly wasted space. Here it has been put to good use with the addition of a desk, which, with its gothic ornamentation, fits in well with the classical lines of the four poster. A strong lipstick red on the walls is echoed in the patterned fabric and the candlelamp shades. The simple cream calico used around the bed is finished off with a co-ordinating border and although the bed is a mix of textures, the overall effect is remarkably unfussy.

Contemporary

Contemporary bedrooms are often as much about atmosphere and style as drawing ideas from the strictly modern movement. For instance, a bedroom sparsely furnished with a few pieces of the simple wooden Shaker furniture, designed over two hundred years ago, can look every bit as contemporary as a pure minimalist design using the latest in twentieth-century technology.

What is interesting about the bedroom as a room is how the vast majority of us actually want something easy to live with: gentle, inviting, comforting, even feminine. The tendency towards frills and flounces under these circumstances is understandable, but there is no reason why those with a desire for something a little more contemporary should not manage to combine a clean, modern approach with all the creature comforts. While the contemporary bedroom is obviously not a place for the unashamedly feminine – fussy festoons or

ornate furniture – neither does it have to be cold, clinical or spartan. The point about taking the modern approach is that there is no room for clutter. These bedrooms are simple and unadorned. This is not the place for indulgent displays of personal possessions, for eclectic collections of photos in frames or mementoes of past holidays arranged higgledy-piggledy on a chest of drawers. In a contemporary bedroom, for example, family photos will be shown off in identical frames and hung on the wall in strict order so that the whole arrangement, rather than just one frame at a time, becomes the focus of attention.

Bedrooms

Flooring will often set the tone for the contemporary bedroom. Simple wooden strips, well polished and maintained, make the perfect foil for the clean lines of modern furniture. Rugs are very much at home in this environment, but they will be positioned rather than scattered: at the side of the bed or in front of a chest of drawers. Equally, a natural flooring would be a good choice, but keep the texture as simple as possible. Carpet is a warm and endlessly varied alternative for your modern room. If the look you want is one of simple, pale tones, then opt for an unobtrusive colour. On the other hand, there are some wonderfully strong modern colours available these days, as well as excellent carpets with good border designs that would fit well into a bold scheme.

The bed is likely to be the main focus in a contemporary bedroom. It could be a low-lying futon or mattress, which would automatically give the room an Oriental flavour. At the other extreme, you might consider a modern four-poster bed where the simple struts are made of wrought iron and hung either with plain muslin, or perhaps entirely unadorned. Don't feel your choice of bed has to be limited to the strictly modern. Equally at home in this environment would be an antique wooden bed, provided that it was of a simple design, with unadorned bedhead and dressed in plain fabrics.

The Shaker look, with simple blue-and-white checked bedlinen, is entirely appropriate in a contemporary bedroom, provided that the rest of the furnishings are fairly plain and unembellished.

Colour plays an important role in the contemporary bedroom – even if it is predominantly white. There are two approaches when it comes to colour: the bold and the unobtrusive. Both have their place, depending on whether you want the overall impact of your room to be dazzling or calm, whether you want background relief against which you can set off your furniture and objects to greatest effect, and whether you want colour to be the dominating force in the room.

It is most likely that you will use paints and colour-washes to achieve your desired effect. You might even consider colouring your walls using paints based on traditional materials and pigments: rich earthy colours, for instance, of ochre and umber, or perhaps the bright Mediterranean tones from Turkey and Greece. Whilst this is not the place for fussy stencils or paint effects, you might find that bold repetitions of strong geometric designs such as a stencilled border would fit in well with your overall design.

Having said that the contemporary bedroom is not the place for clutter, we all manage to produce lots of it. This means that storage in a modern design is one of the key considerations. Before you get involved in purchasing any cupboards or chests, make a list of everything that you might have to put behind doors or into drawers so that

your requirements are accurately met. If you are lucky enough to have the space, then a run of fitted cupboards would be ideal. To stay contemporary, these might be designed as simple flat-fronted panels which would cleverly conceal the doors behind which no end of clothes and clutter can be hidden away.

The Shakers loved quantities of drawers for storage. If you are taking the simple wooden approach, then one of their huge cases of drawers in elegant cherry wood would be perfect for sorting and storing everything from clothes to jewellery to make-up. For clothes, a lower chest of drawers with a simple flat front, perhaps in cherry or maple, would be perfect. And these days there is no end to the ranges of brighter, slightly zanier storage. If there is not much room in your bedroom, then you might consider an aluminium frame hung around with brightly-coloured canvas behind which you can neatly store endless possessions. Even simple storage boxes can be very effective, perhaps painted in complementary colours and stacked systematically.

The windows in a contemporary bedroom can boast a variety of treatments. Simple wooden louvre shutters will instantly give most rooms a cleaner line, and the way they allow the sunshine to slant into a room is most effective. Roman blinds are another functional alternative. If you want curtains, ensure that they are designed with crisp, clean lines and unfussy pelmets. A curtain at its simplest could be a sheet of cream muslin hung off a metal pole and falling in folds on the floor – a thoroughly modern, yet feminine approach.

Your bed linen will also be a key to the contemporary look. Comfort and warmth is every bit as important here as in a traditional room. The only difference is that the design of bedclothes you choose will be less adorned. Vast square pillows with plain white cotton cases, and piled high on a bed, look just as inviting as their frilly counterparts. Throws in simple weaves or plain coloured blankets are every bit as hospitable as their traditional alternatives. Indeed, the jewel-like colours of some of the traditional blankets being produced today lend themselves perfectly to a contemporary setting, without sacrificing any quality or warmth.

Keep your accessories on show to a minimum; just a few carefully chosen objects will suffice. Modern ceramics, or one astonishing lamp will keep the style of the room tightly focused.

With the right ingredients and approach your contemporary bedroom will make a strong style statement, and will be every bit as much of a sanctuary, a comfort and a pleasure to be in as its traditional counterpart.

Be warned: in a house like this every single little detail counts. Here the bedhead is actually a fixed architectural feature that wittily mirrors the lines created by the railings in the landing. The simplest of white walls allows the pale wood, galvanized metal and wire threads to make the impact. There is no necessity for decorative accessories, and certainly no colour. The self-pattern on the white cotton bedspread is the only appropriate ornamentation.

Above: In this elegantly contemporary bedroom the four-poster bed, chest of drawers and side tables come from the Shaker range of furniture by Grange. The clean lines of the bed's canopy need little adornment and the plain white walls provide the perfect foil for the bold colours and shapes that give this room its modern feel. Top: An idiosyncratic collection of black objects gives this room a Hollywood feel. The white background shows off their clean lines to best advantage

Despite the fact that this room uses many traditional design influences such as the glass-topped table, fabric-covered walls, and bergère chair they have been given a contemporary interpretation. The discipline of using just one colour immediately changes the emphasis, and a series of Roman blinds at the window gives the room a distinct sense of line. Right: Small quantities of lace are perfectly acceptable in the contemporary room provided the other accessories are simple.

This room under the eaves gets all the ornament and shape it needs from the lines of the roof and the pattern created by the concealed cupboard doors in the wall. The combination of taupe, grey and white is most effective in producing an interior that is both strictly contemporary yet warm and welcoming. The generous futon bed boasts giant square pillows with simple white covers, and the waffle bedspread adds a strong texture. The floor is painted and varnished.

Part of a high-ceilinged room has been converted into a modest mezzanine bedroom. Here the plain wooden bed frame gives this area an almost oriental simplicity. The floorboards were in good enough condition to be sanded and painted in a bone-coloured wash to complete the feeling of a shell-like space. The strongest focal point comes from the painting with its bold blue vase, which is echoed by the one placed on the low bedside table and again by the blue lines of the chair.

The black frame in the centre of this wall is given an intense clarity thanks to the mellow colours and materials that surround it. Built-in maple alcove wardrobes, designed by McFadden Cabinetmakers, are connected by a headboard which serves as a convenient shelf for bedside clutter. The ticking duvet cover and blue silk cushions maintain the strict order here whilst the apricot walls and glowing lamps ensure that there is nothing spartan about the room.

Brave, bold colour is the key to giving this plumply inviting bedroom its contemporary appeal. The matt-finish heliotrope combines boldness with a surprising warmth. The bed is housed in a shallow alcove created by the fitted cupboards and bedside tables. A hotch-potch of blue fabrics pick out the swag. Right: The vaulted ceiling was the inspiration for the rest of this bedroom, which uses pale blue and white as the only colours to create this beautifully airy sanctuary.

There is a strong Mediterranean theme to this bedroom. The ingredients are simple: walls that are colour-washed in a gentle powder blue; the simplest of wrought-iron bed frames; matching blue muslin draped from a central point and a simple cotton rug on the floor. The duvet and pillows are covered in Mallory Stripe by Laura Ashley. Left: This is a marvellously disciplined room. Plush fabrics, heavy drapes and little adornment, give a clean, modern look.

There is no reason why those with a desire for a more contemporary bedroom should not manage to combine an up-to-date approach with all the creature comforts. This bedroom has a thoroughly feminine ambience, yet at the same time the simple combination of colours together with elegant lines give it a present-day appeal. The broad pink-and-white striped fabric is the key to this room. The witty oriental-shaped pelmet brings a touch of the East to this room.

A country cottage need not fall into the ubiquitous frills and flounces routine. Here brave red-and-white checks have been combined with a quite differently proportioned lining to create a strong visual impact. The bed fills the room but, thanks to the delicate frame, manages not to overpower the space. The lines of the canopy are matched by the wrought-iron curtain pole, and the less obtrusive sprigged fabric is used again at the window. The walls are kept bare for simplicity.

This room shows total colour confidence. The flat, tomato-red paint is the perfect background to set off the vast range of strong textures and tones within. Heavy wickerwork, kilims and woven cotton throws are from the Kenya Range of furniture at The Pier. Rugs placed on top of a natural flooring will make the path underfoot a little softer. Right: Sometimes it is simply the choice of bedlinen that creates the feel of a room. Here an explosion of pinks gives real impact.

The positioning of the bed takes advantage of these gloriously elegant French windows and the view beyond. The polished wooden floor and simple muslin screen give this unquestionably classical room a clean, contemporary balance. A gilt-framed mirror rests on the marble fireplace, but other than this, the walls require no embellishment. The wooden floor continues into the en-suite bathroom where a latticed panel and blue-and-white blind maintain the decorating theme.

Mixing checks of different proportion, and indeed colour, has become an up-to-date way of working with traditional fabrics. This combination immediately looks modern, clean and fresh. The contemporary wicker chair serves as a bedside table, and this owner is lucky enough still to have the original wooden shutters which can remain uncluttered by fabric curtains. Right: This pretty, modern interpretation of a classical country-house bedroom is put together by Laura Ashley.

Despite the fact that it was designed over two hundred years ago, Shaker furniture can look every bit as contemporary as anything designed today. Using just a few carefully selected pieces, the look is minimalist, elegant and up to the minute. These items in maple and cherry wood come from Shaker in London. Combined with the homespun blue-and-white check fabric-covered chair and the unsophisticated cotton weave rug, the room has an enviably unaffected appeal that is timeless.

Babies, Childr

Children spend a great deal of time in their bedrooms and this places enormous demands on it to be a space that is versatile, safe and yet fun to be in. For babies the demands on a bedroom will tend to be geared towards the requirements of adults, ensuring the room is adequately set up for feeding, nappy changing and possibly even bathing. Later, a toddler will start to collect toys of all shapes and sizes and at that point storage and safety become an issue. He may, even at this early stage, have strong ideas about what the bedroom should look like. Then as the child grows up there must be space for homework, desks, self expression, hobbies, and perhaps even a computer, stereo or television.

Versatility is the key to any successful children's room: a design simple enough to grow with the child. It is so tempting when your baby is tiny to fall into the pale pastels and fluffy bunny trap. Unless you're happy to redecorate quickly, resist. Before you know it, your baby will be well past the fluffy bunny stage and you, as well as the child, will wish you'd chosen something more appropriate that can be adapted to your child's changing requirements.

The bedroom is the perfect place for a child to journey into his imagination and you should aim for this room to be every bit the private sanctuary for your child that your own room is for you. Children's needs change rapidly as they grow but by the time a child is three years you will probably have a very good idea of the sort of bedroom they want. Be it princess-pretty or decorated with bright murals – you can be

n, Teens

sure that it will be quite distinctive. To maintain the impact of your chosen design, storage is probably the most important element in a successful children's room. It should aim to be both practical and fun – you will be much more likely to keep a toddler's bedroom neat and tidy if your child actually enjoys putting things away.

From the very beginning try to think ahead. Your baby may only want a little chest of drawers for the small clothes, and somewhere to store the nappies and changing paraphernalia, but, before you know it, the baby nighties will be replaced by bulkier jeans, sweatshirts and dresses on hangers – all of which take up a great deal of room. It is certainly worth planning ahead so that you don't buy dainty furniture that soon becomes redundant, meaning further expenditure on more substantial items.

In the same way, the line up of soft toys will very quickly be joined by bigger, awkwardly-shaped toys which will need somewhere to live. Boxed games in particular need wide enough shelving, or concealing cupboards, to avoid messy, toppling towers of toys. By the time your child is three or four you may well be astonished at the number of books that have amassed and which need adequate shelf space.

Consider putting up shelving systems on metal track so that the height of the shelves can be altered to suit a child's growing needs. Be as generous as possible with the length and number of shelves. You may not fill them up immediately but you will one day. You can then use the shelves that can be reached by your child for books and favourite toys

and those higher up for displaying old soft toys. Look for inexpensive square baskets and use them to house smaller bits and pieces like Lego or collections of cars or dolls. These can then be put out of the way on the shelves each night. You can buy primary-coloured plastic containers, or you might even like to paint the baskets in different bright colours. A wardrobe in which the height of the hanging rails can be altered is another good purchase as this will grow with your child.

Once your child has moved from a cot to bed, there is another chance for more storage with drawers underneath the bed for spare bedclothes or toys and games. Many divans have inbuilt drawers, or you can buy large free-standing wooden drawers that fit snugly under any bed. They can easily be hidden by a valance to keep the room looking neat. This is a very useful piece of storage, particularly if you have more than one child in the bedroom, as the drawer under each bed gives each child very important areas of delineation as to their own property.

Consider storage that will see a child right through to his teens. You cannot go wrong with a chest of drawers, blanket chest, a system of adjustable shelving and a wardrobe from the beginning. The only addition to this will be some sort of desk system with adequate storage for the child once he needs to do homework in peace and quiet, or to pursue his hobbies.

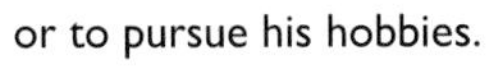

Colour and pattern plays an enormous role in the development of any child. Most children, even small babies, respond better to bright strong colours than to pastel shades, but this does not mean that you have to produce a garish, unpalatable scheme. Introduce the bold colour with accessories – perhaps a large, bright rug, or curtains with a strong pattern. Hang big posters on the walls. Great fun can be had with witty paint effects – polka dots on the mantlepiece, wobbly stripes below a dado rail or on the skirting, or uneven checks painted on the door.

There is no doubt that whatever your child chooses at three years old he will have moved on to another phase several years later. Making good use from the beginning of elements that can be changed quickly and easily – a paint finish, for instance, or curtains or blinds – will totally change the atmosphere in a room to suit a new stage in a child's development.

Unless you don't mind replacing expensive items like the bed every few years, think carefully before buying gimmicky furniture. A bed that looks like a bus, for instance, may be great fun at four, but bear in mind that your ten-year-old may feel too grown up for it. A more flexible solution would be to get a good-quality single bed that will last for years, and cartoon-character bedlinen can be replaced with more adult designs relatively cheaply. The bedhead can be painted with a fun design to start with and then repainted in a more sophisticated way later on.

If you have space, a comfortable armchairwill suit a breastfeeding mother, later provide a cosy spot for listening to bedtime stories, and will finally suit the child who can read to himself.

Lighting should be as simple as possible, and either easy for a toddler to turn on himself, or safely positioned out of his reach. Older children who like to read in bed will want a bedside lamp; choose one with a sturdy base so that it does not get knocked over. For homework, make sure the desk lamp is bright enough to avoid headaches or eyestrain. And remember that many children like the comfort and security of a soft nightlight.

At the windows, there are a number of options. Roman blinds are a good choice if your fabric has a pictorial pattern that needs to be seen in one go. Blackout blinds or curtains with a black backing are extremely useful if your children are early risers.

Involve your child in all these decisions, allowing him or her the chance to make an important contribution to the look of their room.

This room is clearly intended to grow with the child. The combination of spots on the wall and checks on the sofa, both in the brightest of yellow, ensures a friendly, jolly atmosphere in which any child would enjoy spending time. This scheme would, however, see the child right through to its teens and beyond without any embarrassment. Boxes covered in a selection of fabrics make simple toy storage. The animal fabric on the cushions combines childish appeal with elegance.

This bedroom may be small, but it manages to combine amazing amounts of storage with versatility of use. Every available shelf space has been used for display. Under the bed, storage drawers are hidden by a simple checked valance. A piece of padding along the side of the bed turns it instantly into a sofa, and the bedside table is also a writing desk. Simple fabrics make this room suitable for boy or girl and without doubt the perfect private sanctuary for its owner.

Thinking ahead ensures that there is adequate storage in your child's room. The line-up of soft toys when a baby is born is rapidly increased in just a few years. Built-in units, from floor to ceiling, house those that are not in use higher up, and current favourites within easy reach. A generous armchair is the perfect place for two or more to cuddle up for bedtime stories. Right: Stripes are the perennial favourite for a child's room. A chest of drawers will see your child through to his teens.

This baby's room has been designed to cater for all the early functions, such as feeding, changing and long day-time naps. The fabrics and wallpaper, from Designers' Guild, prove that strong, bold patterns work every bit as well as pastels in a nursery. The nappy changing is done on a neat piece of furniture designed by the owner, and the small glass-fronted unit houses all the necessary bits and pieces. This is a room that any new mother would be happy to spend a lot of time in.

Colour and pattern play an enormous role in the development of any child. Most children, even small babies, respond better to bright, strong colours than to pastel shades. Great fun can be had with witty paint effects. In this room the pattern on the wallpaper is echoed with the polka dots on the mantelpiece. These are easily done with a sponge cut to the right size and shape. A small unit houses storage baskets and boxes. These are easy to put away and look fun, too.

This room has been thoroughly thought out to cater to any child's needs. A low shelving unit runs the length of one wall, giving display and work space on top, and easily accessible storage space below. Part of the unit has been turned into a simple dolls' house using basic cupboard doors. There is plenty of space on the walls to display the many works of art and a table for craft activities. The easy-to-clean floor tiles are matched by the bright-yellow window surround.

There can be no greater encouragement for a child than to be given a huge area for diplaying his or her own precious artwork. A simple pinboard fills one wall of this bedroom and the frame has been painted in a bright yellow that adds to the sunny colour scheme. Right: This pretty little sleigh bed is from Harriet Ann Beds, and the wall has been painted to look like the sky by Helena Laidlaw in Flax Blue vinyl by Sanderson. A perfect haven for a small girl.

A fresh yellow-and-blue colour scheme is ideal for a small child, and will still appeal as he or she grows. This capacious yellow-painted shelving unit clearly shows the versatility of its differently sized sections. Books may eventually fill all the shelves, but for now they fit comfortably at the bottom. A collection of favourite teddy bears is displayed, alternating with woven baskets that can hide all manner of more frequently used bits and pieces.

An explosion of pattern and colour in this room provides a marvellously rich environment for any child. The simple roller blinds are embellished with strips of pennant flags made of different fabrics. The unusually shallow gap between window sill and skirting has been taken advantage of with a co-ordinating wallpaper border. The pelmet for the roller blinds provides a useful display shelf away from little hands. A bedside light is important for older children.

This is unquestionably a little boy's room and yet it manages not to be too insensitively stereotyped. Checks, tartans and racing cars from the Nursery Window combine pell mell to create a riot of colours and textures which are excellent in disguising the inevitable wear and tear. A smart, checked duvet cover and flat-pleated valance ensure that whilst this room is pleasing to the eye, it would never embarrass the most masculine of little boys.

A sophisticated fabric such as *toile de jouy* looks utterly appropriate in a child's room, particularly if combined, as here, with the simple pink stripes hand-painted on to the wall. An antique patchwork bedspread, natural coir matting and oriental fireside rug suit the timeless appeal of this room. The gothic panels in the fitted cupboards provide yet more visual stimulus. This room would double-up equally well as a guest bedroom.

These colours may be gentle on the eye, but there is nothing sickly or pastel about them – far from it. A thoroughly inviting combination of fabrics: linen at the window, soft wool blankets, and a natural cotton rug ensure that this room can easily be converted from nursery, through toddler's room, right to the teenage years if necessary. Fabric curtains hung in front of a shelving unit are a pretty way to hide any unsightly paraphernalia. A big basket stores toys.

Storage & Disp

Despite the fact that storage and display require very different solutions, they are undoubtedly part of the same dilemma. Whether you are displaying your favourite possessions, or trying to hide away unsightly clutter, you will need to tackle the question of what type of furniture or fitment you require to do either job best.

Lucky is the person who doesn't accumulate more bedroom clutter than they can accommodate. A quick look around your own room will reveal no end of magazines, piles of books, spare pillows and blankets, overnight bags or suitcases, and even dirty laundry. Storage solutions need to be carefully thought out before embarking on major purchases. The most important rule is to go for more storage capacity than you think is required. You will almost definitely use it.

Chests of drawers, wardrobes and dressing tables are the most obvious items for bedroom storage. If you do

not have enough room for bulky free-standing cupboards, take a leaf out of the Shakers' books. They built whole walls of fitted wardrobes, which had plenty of hanging space and endless drawers to satisfy even the greatest storage requirements. Plan in advance exactly what you are going to put into each cupboard, so that you can customize the inside to suit your needs.

Outside, the doors can be designed to suit any bedroom decoration: ornately panelled for a traditional room, or with a plain, unbeaded front for a sleeker, contemporary look. Mirrored panels can break the dominant look of

ay

a wall of doors, while also creating the illusion of space and providing a useful full-length looking-glass.The handles you choose will also dramatically alter the effect your cupboards have upon the room. If you are going to paint the doors, try to avoid shiny white gloss, and choose instead a matt finish – a pretty colour-wash, for instance, that blends with the walls or the curtain fabric you have chosen. A gently distressed finish can be very effective in helping a long run of fitted wardrobes seem less obtrusive.

But there are other less obvious places to hide your untidiness. A table, given a simple material skirt, makes invaluable storage space for clutter such as piles of magazines, shoes or even books which can be hidden behind the fabric. Bedside tables designed with cupboard space are also invaluable for keeping all sorts of possessions out of sight.

Blanket chests or upholstered ottomans are one marvellous solution to the problems of spare bedding, clothes currently out of use, and other bits and pieces that need to be instantly out of sight. And of course they also serve a double purpose as useful seating.

A decorative way to store small items is to use old hatboxes, which can be stacked on top of a wardrobe or on shelves. They can be covered in fabric or coloured paper to suit the decoration of the room. The Shakers, again, had their own simple stacking-box system: brightly painted versions of their elegant oval boxes can easily be found. Equally successful in this capacity are old leather suitcases which will add an attractive, weatherbeaten look to a country-

style or traditional bedroom. For a more contemporary look you could even adapt office storage systems. Different sized durable cardboard stacking boxes are now widely available in a range of colours.

Displaying, rather than hiding, some bedroom clutter can be a way of turning storage to your advantage. Shaker-style pegs on the wall, for instance, are a good way to tidy up odd pieces of clothing, hats, scarves and even long necklaces, and seem to elevate messy clutter to the ranks of decoration instantly. In a small room, in which you seem to have little scope for display, look for 'dead space' to utilize. The tops of wardrobes, for instance, can house pretty baskets, which in turn usefully conceal iteams better hidden.

If you are meticulously tidy, then open-plan shelves can be an extremely effective way of storing jumpers or shirts – few people are so finicky that they are prepared to spend the time arranging their clothes by colour, but as long as things are stowed away neatly this can look good. There are now numerous aids to good storage for sale in the shops: interesting honeycomb-shaped drawer inserts for keeping socks and tights in order; lengths of small canvas pigeonholes on hangers which can help hide away no end of small objects inside your wardrobe or behind a door; and vast ranges of differently-shaped boxes, covered in plain or patterned fabrics, all of which would look good stacked on shelves or on the top of cupboards.

Displaying your favourite possessions is always a pleasurable job. Collections of treasured objects take years to build up and you will want to display them to maximum benefit. The glorious thing about any well-loved collection is that it is often a lifetime's work and consequently is never static but always changing and being added to. Even an informal display can be given cohesion by a common theme, and, with prints or photographs, similarly styled frames.

The key is to arrange things so that they fit with the decorative style of the room and also so that they are put in the optimum position to set them off to advantage. Consider carefully which pieces you want to display together and then find the right setting. Glass, for instance, will pick up and reflect all the subtle changes in light if you place it by a window. Reflecting the theme of your collection in fabric and furnishings also makes an impact. The botanical flavour of the room on page 72 for example, is echoed not only in the prints, but in the fabric, and the painted dec-

oration on the chest of drawers. Take care not to dwarf small items. They need a display space that makes them look significant – a small pigeonhole-style cabinet, either free-standing or hung on the wall would be ideal.

Rugs don't have to go on the floor. If you have a strong collection of similar styles, try hanging them from your wall instead. A set of antique plates – they don't have to match – can make a very bold statement when hung on the wall of a traditionally-decorated bedroom. When massing paintings or prints together, try to group them thematically. They certainly don't have to be the same size, although colour, period or style can be a good way to group them. Lie them out on the floor before hanging so that you can fit the different sizes alongside each other to make a satisfactory overall shape on the wall.

In a contemporary bedroom it can be very effective to have pictures or photographs shown off in identical frames hung in straight lines, perhaps three lines of three frames. Small objects, perhaps shells, or interesting seaweed from a beach holiday, will be given a new dimension by being displayed individually in simple box-frames and hung on the wall, rather than gathering dust on the top of a mantlepiece. The contemporary look is enhanced by displays of the 'less is more' variety. Choose a few strong pieces to create an impact without destroying the room's simplicity.

Remember, bookcases don't have to be for books alone. You can create interesting still-lives by being more imaginative: a few books, a vase, maybe a small object all on one shelf will look far more tantalizing, and you can change the mix as often as you want.

This potentially monotonous line of fitted cupboards is broken by the two glass-panelled doors in the centre, which instantly provide an attractive visual focus. This combination by Smallbone of Devizes offers plenty of storage space and accommodates long and short hanging units and drawers. When planning an expensive fitted option such as this always aim for more storage capacity than you think is required. You will unquestionably use it.

In a small bedroom fitted cupboards can often be the simplest of storage solutions, but they can also be a little too dominant. Mirrored panels are the answer as they fulfil several functions at once. An effective looking-glass, the reflection also creates a feeling of space by doubling the size of the room. Here, gothic arches are the simple point of interest. Right: A collection of blue plates are carefully arranged on the wall in a shape that echoes the bedhead.

The top of a wardrobe can often seem like dead space, yet this can be the perfect place for displaying, rather than hiding, certain pieces of clutter. A collection of old leather suitcases, or, indeed, wicker baskets (below and right) can house an inordinate amount of objects: old magazines, clothes, shoes, letters and the like. These can then be grouped together, one on top of the other for emphasis. Suddenly clutter has been elevated to the ranks of decoration.

This tiny dressing room designed and decorated by Dido Farrell manages to ingeniously accommodate each item so that everything is easy to see at a glance and instantly accessible. A space like this is surely the dream for most of us. If you are meticulously tidy you can turn the lack of cupboard doors into a decorating virtue using the shape and colour of your clothes to create visual impact. A pair of speakers are hidden behind the cut-out stars and moon.

This freestanding maple unit was designed by McFadden Cabinetmakers. It was originally designed for a bathroom but works just as well in the bedroom. Plenty of shallow drawers make items easier to locate. Right: The joy of freestanding cupboards is that they go wherever you go. On top of this, they allow flexibility in the arrangement of any room because you can move them. This ordinary little cupboard has been elevated by its paint and stencil finish.

A matching pair of bookshelves have been fitted to hang from the ceiling down, on either side of the magnificent bed panel. This has the effect of turning them into an integral part of the *trompe l'oeil* and thus into a strong display element. Fabric-covered ottomans are a marvellous solution to the problems of storage. Inside the elegant little boxes, which also serve as useful extra seating, you can hide away from sight endless clobber, yet still retain instant access.

This elegant cameo has its roots in Gustavian design with the pale, colourwashed cabinet and chairs. The classically simple symmetry is achieved with the pair of chairs, one either side of the unit and, at a higher level, the matching lamps on top. Interestingly, the object that pulls the whole display together is the pewter tray, positioned off centre. The result is that this eclectic group of objects – a soup tureen, small glass and tray – is displayed to full advantage.

No gentleman's dressing room is complete without a set of cedar-lined shelves on which to stack shirts neatly. These slimline units have simple, glass-panelled doors backed unobtrusively by plain, gathered material. Four pictures with an equestrian theme are displayed in a neat arrangement around the clock, which has become the central point of focus. The rosette succeeds in linking the disparate elements on the wall and turning the whole into one strong, visual display.

Flowers provide the unifying theme in this refreshingly pretty corner of a bedroom. The otherwise plain Victorian chest of drawers has been skilfully drawn into the composition by painting it in a co-ordinating colour and copying the fabric's rose motif on to three of the drawers. The large botanical prints make this a perfect bedroom for a gardener. Right: Storage can be turned into a virtue by using different fabric sacks to put away anything from underwear to bathroom towels.

This informal arrangement of botanical prints still manages to maintain some sense of order and is saved from seeming twee with the addition of one large print hung on the adjacent wall. The display in this picture shows how an overall cohesion has been achieved with frames of varying sizes simply because there is a subject matter and frame design common to all the prints. A small occasional table has been turned into a pretty bedside display area.

A veneered cherrywood chest of drawers from the Consulat range by Grange allows this interesting collection of objects to be displayed at the perfect height. The mellow colour of the wood sets off the stark black of the two oxen and the whole ensemble is arranged from left to right in height order. The formality of this grouping is broken by the addition of the chunky necklaces. The white walls look crisp but not stark in this African-themed room.

The owner of this house has turned the attic space into an ingenious storage and dressing area. The many small drawers in the chemist's-shop chest provide generously for endless storage and the top serves as a dressing table. With two clothes rails on either side of the room this clever use of space has created a simple walk-in wardrobe. Left: It is all too easy to dwarf small items on display. They need a unit that makes them seem significant, such as this little shelf unit.

Basics

If your bedroom is to be the haven you hope for, then it is important to get the basics right from the beginning. When it comes to planning and buying them, it is the decorative basics such as headboards and bedlinens that most of us think about first, simply because, being visible, they play such an enormous role in the way the bedroom looks.

But it is astonishing how many people choose to skimp on the most fundamental basics of all – the mattress on which you will sleep, the pillows and the duvet – simply because they don't add anything to the decorative quality of the bedroom and, frequently, they are surprisingly expensive.

We spend around a third of our lives in bed. Most couples sleep on a 135cm (4ft 6in) bed which only provides 68cm (2ft 3in) of space for each person – only slightly wider than a baby's cot. It is reckoned that we toss and turn as much as seventy times during the night. Add to that the fact that most of us are sleeping on mattresses badly suited either to our weight or our backs, and it is hardly surprising that both partners may suffer from disturbed sleep.

You can expect a new bed to last around ten years. It is an important purchase, yet most of us merely bounce on the edge of a mattress to test its suitability in the shop. This is not satisfactory. The National Bed Federation offers clear guidelines on bed buying and insist that it is essential you adopt your normal sleeping position when testing potential new beds. The NBF suggests that you should spend at least ten minutes on each prospective new bed. You should lie on your back and slide the flat of

your hand between the small of your back and the mattress. If there is a gap between your back and the mattress the bed is too firm. If the small of your back is filled with the mattress and you have difficulty sliding your hand in, it is too soft. You should be able to put your hand under your back and feel the mattress gently responding to your shape and supporting you.

Don't fall into the trap of believing that 'hard' is good. Many people with bad backs rush to buy an 'orthopaedic' mattress, thinking that this will cure the problem. Although a new bed that keeps the spine in current alignment may give instant relief, it can be an expensive mistake to buy an orthopaedic bed only to discover that it is impossibly firm, and actually aggravates a back condition. If you already own a mattress that is too hard, many companies now produce a soft top layer, either foam or fibre-filled, which you can put on the top.

The inside of a mattress can be a mystery to many of us. As a general guide, pocket-spring mattresses are more luxurious than open-spring designs, as they have better quality fillings and finishings. Some companies, Heal's for instance, still produce mattresses with traditional fillings such as animal hair or sheep's wool. Some of their designs have no internal springs and rely on the natural fillings to provide comfort and support.

You will also have other considerations, when buying a mattress, if you suffer from allergies. Approximately four million people suffer from asthma, and fewer than half of them realize that their bed may be aggravating their problems. Many people have a strong allergic reaction to feathers, hair and wool, although the main culprit is the house dustmite, a microscopic animal that feeds on dead skin. Since we lose up to half a kilo (1 lb) of skin a year – much of this in bed – the warm, moist environment of a bed is the perfect habitat for dustmites. If your mattress is over ten years old, it will not only be worn out but also contain a decade's worth of allergen-laden dustmite dung.

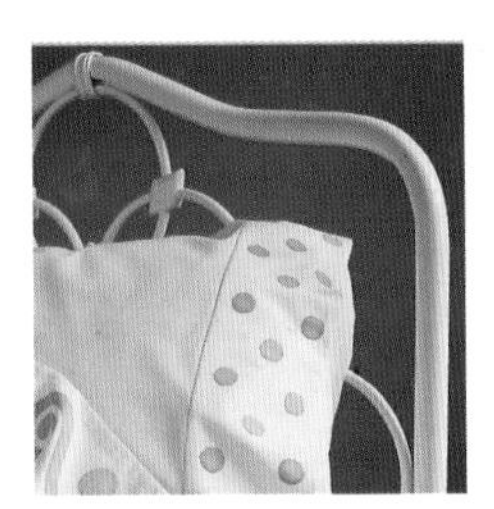

Asthma sufferers should consider a wooden or metal bedstead, where dust is less likely to accumulate, and a latex or foam mattress. As an added precaution, use a non-fabric mattress cover, choose synthetic-filled duvets and pillows, and wash your bedding every week at 60° centigrade, as this temperature kills dustmites.

For real comfort, you might even consider one of the new adjustable beds that provide numerous sleep, relaxing or reading positions at the flick of a switch.

Once you have found the ultimate mattress you can turn your attentions to the bedhead. Any design you choose will play an essential role in shaping the overall style and look of the bedroom. The range of possibilities is so vast that you must think about your own comfort and requirements before making any decision.

For instance, if you enjoy reading in bed, or indulging in lazy weekend breakfasts, then it would be unwise to opt for a hard carved wood headboard or, indeed, one of the delicately caned variety. Upholstered headboards are not only extremely comfortable to sit up against, but thanks to the limitless prospects of fabric covering, they will suit any colourway and design style. It's even possible to find headboards that combine the elegance of wood with a comfortable padded back.

If you want your bed to be the most dominant factor in the room, then a four poster, or the French *lit bateau* will do the job magnificently. Four posters lend themselves to a variety of different looks, and need not be heavily curtained. The exotic, Eastern feel of the bed on page 83 is created by hanging it with saris. Equally, a quite unimposing bed can be made to look positively regal with the addition of a corona – a small, semi-circular piece of wood, positioned on the wall above the bed from which fabric is draped.

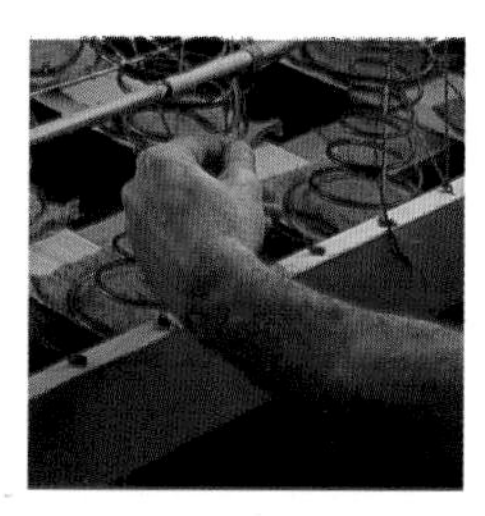

Some bedheads, of course, are made for particular environments: antique brass or metal for instance, is utterly appropriate for a traditional, cottage-style room, simple, unadorned fruitwood is just right for a room decked out in country checks and stripes, and many plain bedheads can compliment the contemporary look.

Finally, what you put on to your bed will make all the difference to the pleasure you feel when you get between the sheets. For most of us, the ultimte luxury is pure linen – but not if you are the one who has to wash and iron it. When choosing sheets and duvet covers, the range of fabrics can seem awesome. Pure cotton is cool and crisp; although for ease of ironing Percale is a very strong favourite for many people. Some of the best-quality Percale can feel smoother and more inviting than cotton. You may love the pattern of your duvet cover and want to leave it as it is, or prefer to cover it with a bedspread.

Several decades after the conversion to the convienience of duvets, there has been something of a resurgence in the use of sheets and blankets in the last few years, and many woollen mills are now producing traditionally made blankets in gloriously vibrant colours, checks and tartans.

For sheer timelessness, you can't beat plain white bedlinen, perhaps combined with a woollen throw to add a touch of colour. A scattering of cushions can also heighten a plain colour scheme. And in the end the wonderful thing about your bedlinen is that you can change it with your mood and as often as your purse will allow.

A light, airy bedroom such as this benefits from a delicate, less imposing bedhead. The caned panel painted by Helena Laidlaw allows sunlight to filter on to the occupant in a most gentle manner. The colours of both furniture and bedclothes have been carefully chosen with the exterior view in mind: harmonious shades of heather, moss and cream blend perfectly with the natural colours outside. Right: The fresh pink-and-white checks pull together the strong colours in this room.

If you are a breakfast-in-bed addict, then consider carefully the bedhead you choose. A padded, fabric-covered one such as this is undoubtedly the most comfortable to lean against. Blue and white is an abiding colour combination for a fresh, feminine look. Here the countrified patchwork quilt combines perfectly with the floral design on the bedhead to produce an unobstrustive colour scheme that is co-ordinated without being fussy in the slightest.

It does not take much to give your bed a starring role in the room. The impact of this example comes primarily from the strong use of just one fabric which contrasts starkly with the floral wallpaper. Add to that the curvaceous bedhead and the simple, yet regal corona with its modest, tab-headed drapes and the effect is powerful. Right: This charming bed from Simon Horn is in French provincial style and would have been popular during the reign of Louis XVI.

Classic wooden beds are a comforting and substantial addition to any bedroom. This grand *'lit bateau'* is based on a bed originally made by a family in the Auvergne. It has been redesigned by Simon Horn and is now made in the UK from solid French walnut. Right: A ravishing way to turn a simple four poster into a luxuriant sleeping space is to hang it with a selection of richly coloured, golden-threaded saris. The glowing reds add warmth to the grandeur of the room.

The room may be based around neutral colours, but the impact is far from dreary. The crisp, white sheets and pillows are topped with a cotton, self-patterned bedspread and further layered with a honeycomb patchwork quilt bordered with taupe and cream checks. The bedhead has the simplest of covers: fabric-padded on the underside, and held in place with delicate ties at the side. The assortment of cushions in different fabrics is an effortless device that pulls the room together.

This bedhead elegantly combines the attractiveness of painted wood with the comfort of a padded back. Here the owner has created the prettiest country bedroom without falling prey to excessive frills and flounces. The American-style quilt is a perfect decorative cover-up, and strong in its own right, taking nothing away from the gilded bedhead. A quilt of this weight is perfect all year round: a welcome extra layer in winter, and a summer covering that is barely there.

Gathered, pleated, draped and frilled, the many metres of fabric on this four-poster bed certainly work hard to create a sumptuous haven for whoever sleeps here. This is a bedroom that pays total homage to the grand country-house look. No expense is spared to produce an exaggeratedly co-ordinated room that manages to look gentle and pretty as opposed to intimidating. The bedlinen has been carefully chosen not to take anything away from the other fabric.

Marvellously baroque, this caned footboard of a bed by Simon Horn, called *'la Reine de Versaille'*, hardly needs any extra embellishment to make an impact. However, the half-tester, with its witty fabric heading, adds just the right amount of panache and the whole thing makes a truly romantic statement in otherwise unpretentious surroundings. Left: A white-painted iron bedhead is given a contemporary feel with the addition of this embroidered bedlinen from Designers' Guild.

When choosing a bed for your baby it is worth pausing for a moment to think how fast its needs will change over the first few years. The investment in separate cots, beds and different mattresses is potentially enormous. There is more to this cot than meets the eye. Designed by Simon Horn, it is a unique piece of furniture, made of solid cherrrywood, that starts life as a traditional cot, becomes next a bed and then a sofa for a teenager's bedroom.

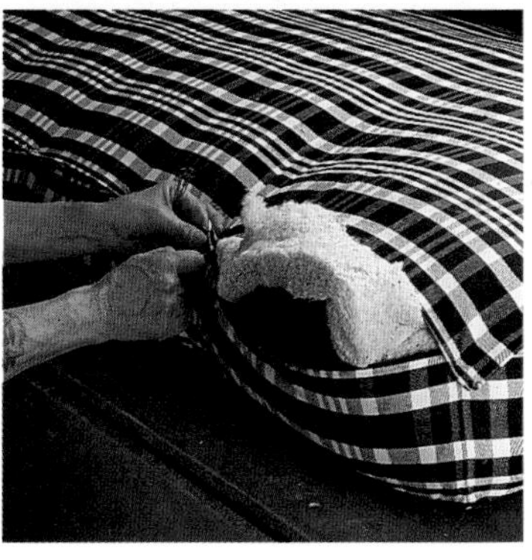

Left: Before the invention of spring mattresses, traditional bedding consisted of hair and fleece stuffed into a fabric bag, hand-stitched to keep the upholstery firmly in place. Heal's still produce such mattresses, based on the portable designs created for the troops in the Crimean War, when they were folded and carried by pack mules. Above right: Installing springs in the base of a bed. Left: Adding the final touches to a hand-made bed.

If you suffer from sleepless nights, a new bed will probably make all the difference. Choosing the right mattress to suit your needs is one of the most important decisions you will make for your bedroom. Considering that you can expect a new bed to last around ten years, it is extraordinary how few of us take this purchase seriously. Follow the National Bed Federation guidelines (see directory for details) and you'll make the right choice.

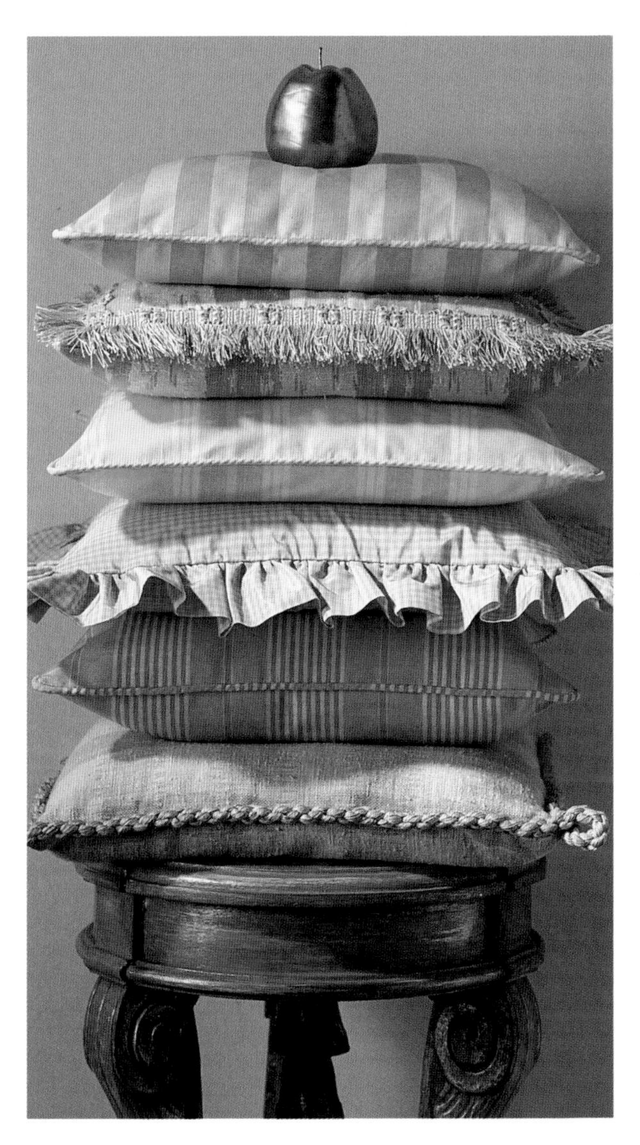

Cushions can be the final decorative touch in any bedroom. A sophisticated selection is shown here in tones of yellow and gold, all made from fabrics by Laura Ashley. This group demonstrates how a simple padded square can be embellished in a variety of ways to suit a vast range of different decorating styles. Right: An eclectic mix of fabrics, colours and styles gel here in a brilliant, unconformist way. Never be afraid to make your own personal statement.

Directory

BEDS

Airsprung Beds, Canal Road Industrial Estate, Trowbridge, Wiltshire BA14 8RQ. Tel. 01225 754411.

The Antique Brass Bedstead Company Ltd, Baddow Antique Centre, Gt Baddow, Chelmsford, Essex CM2 7JW. Tel. 01245 471137.

The Corner Cupboard, 17 King Street, Saffron Walden, Essex. Tel. 01799 526000. A selection of reproduction brass and iron bedsteads, sleigh beds.

Dunlopillo UK, Pannal, Harrogate, North Yorkshire HG3 1JL. Tel. 01423 872411.

The Feather Bed Company, Crosslands House, Ash Thomas, Tiverton, Devon EX16 4NU. Tel. 01884 821331.

The Futon Company. Tel. 0181 995 2271 for nearest branch. A good range of modern bed bases, as well as futons and bedlinen.

Harriet Ann Sleigh Beds, Standen Farm, Smarden Road, Biddenden, Near Ashford, Kent TN27 8JT. Tel. 01580 291220.

Heal & Son, 196 Tottenham Court Road, London W1. Tel. 0171 636 1666. A good range of high-quality beds including their traditionally hand-made beds and mattresses.

The Iron Bed Company, 580 Fulham Road, London SW6 5NT. Tel. 0171 610 9903.

Relyon, Station Mill, PO Box 1, Wellington, Somerset TA21 8NN. Tel. 01823 667501.

Rest Assured, Pontygwaith, Ferndale, Rhondda, Mid Glamorgan CF43 3ED. Tel. 01443 730541.

Royal Auping, 35 Baker Street, London W1M 1AE. Tel. 0171 935 3774 Fax. 0171 935 3720.

Savoy Bedworks, Unit 1, The Willows Centre, 17 Willow Lane, Mitcham, Surrey CR4 4NX. Tel. 0181 648 7701.

Sealy, Station Road, Aspatria, Carlisle, Cumbria CA5 2AS. Tel. 01697 320342.

Simon Horn Furniture, 117/121 Wandsworth Bridge Road, London SW6 2TP. Tel. 0171 731 1279. Examples of their beds can be seen on pages 83, 87 and 88.

Slumberland, Salmon Fields, Royton, Oldham, Lancashire OL2 6SB. Tel. 0161 628 2898.

Vi-Spring Limited, Ernesettle Lane, Ernesettle, Plymouth, Devon PL5 2TT. Tel. 01752 366311. Craftsmade mattresses and beds.

BEDLINEN AND BLANKETS

Anta, 46 Crispin Street, London E1 6QH. Tel. 01862 832477.

Cover-up Designs, Plastow Green, Newbury, Berkshire RG15 8LW. Tel. 01635 23230. Quilted bedspreads, cushions and curtains made to order.

Cologne & Cotton, 74 Regent Street, Leamington Spa, Warwickshire CV32 4NS. Tel. 01926 332573 for mail-order details.

Damask, 3/4 Broxholme House, New King's Road, Nr Harwood Road, London SW6 4AA. Tel. 0171 731 3553. Pretty lace and traditional-style bedlinen.

Descamps, 197 Sloane Street, London SW1X 9QX. Tel. 0171 235 6957. A wide range of traditional and modern bedlinen, duvet covers and quilts.

Designers' Guild, 267/271 & 277 King's Road, London SW3 5EN. Tel. 0171 243 7300. Pure cotton bedlinen, bright modern designs.

Habitat. Tel. 0645 334433 for nearest branch. Good range of bedroom accessories, including bedclothes, duvet covers and curtains.

Jane Churchill, 151 Sloane Street, London SW1X 9BX. Tel. 0171 730 9847. Traditional- and modern-style bedlinen and accessories.
Laura Ashley. Tel. 01628 770345 for nearest branch. See pages 37 and 42 for examples of their bedlinens.
Lunn Antiques, 86 New King's Road, London SW6 4LU. Tel. 0171 736 4638. Antique and modern lace and cotton bedspreads, sheets, pillowcases.
Melin Tregwynt, Tregwynt Mill, Castle Morris, Haverfordwest, Pembrokeshire, Dyfed SA62 5UX. Tel. 01348 891225. Traditionally made wool blankets and throws in a wide range of colours, checks and plains.
Peter Reed. Tel. 01282 692416 for stockists. Fine bedlinens.
The Source. Tel. 01708 890253 for enquiries and information on stores. Well-priced, bright contemporary accessories and bedclothes.

FITTED AND HANDCRAFTED FURNITURE

Hayloft Woodwork, Chiswick, 3 Bond Street, Chiswick, London W4 1QZ. Tel. 0181 747 3510.
Mark Wilkinson, Overton House, High Street, Bromham, Nr Chippenham, Wiltshire SN15 2HA. Tel. 01380 850007. Showrooms also at 126 Holland Park Avenue, London W11 4JA. Tel. 0171 727 5814; 41 St John's Wood High Street, London NW8 7NJ. Tel. 0171 586 9579; 13 Holywell Hill, St Albans, Herts AL1 1EZ. Tel. 01727 840975; 4 High Street, Maidenhead, Berks SL6 1QJ. Tel. 01628 777622; 17 King Street, Knutsford, Cheshire WA16 6DW. Tel. 01565 650800.
McFadden Cabinetmakers, Unit 3, Lymore Gardens, Oldfield Park, Bath BA2 1AQ. Tel. 01225 310593. Bespoke bedroom furniture. See their work on pages 35 and 68.
Rhode Design, 65 Cross Street, London N1 2BB. Tel. 0171 354 9933.
Smallbone of Devizes, 105–109 Fulham Road, London SW3 6RL. Tel. 0171 581 9989. Also showrooms in Knutsford, Devizes, Harrogate, Leamington Spa, Tunbridge Wells.

BEDROOM FURNITURE

Clockhouse Furniture, The Old Stables, Overhailes, Haddington, East Lothian EH41 3SB. Tel. 01620 860968. Traditional fabric-covered stools and ottomans.
The Conran Shop, Michelin House, 81 Fulham Road, London SW3 6RD. Tel. 0171 589 7401.
George Smith, 587/589 King's Road, London SW6 2EH. Tel. 0171 384 1004. Good range of fabric-covered ottomans and armchairs.
Grange, PO Box 18, Stamford, PE9 2FY. Tel. 01780 54721. Fax. 01780 54718. Reproduction French traditional and modern furniture. See pp. 31 & 74.
Habitat. Tel. 0645 334433 for nearest branch. Good range of contemporary and traditional-style beds.
The Pier, 91–95 King's Road, London SW3. Tel. 0171 351 7100. Traditional, ethnic and contemporary bedroom furniture and accessories.
Shaker, 322 King's Road, London SW3. Tel. 0171 352 3918. Traditional Shaker-style furniture and accessories.

FABRICS

Anna French, 343 King's Road, London SW3 5ES. Tel. 0171 351 1126. Co-ordinated fabrics, wallpapers and borders, many based on Victorian designs.
Colefax & Fowler. Tel. 0181 874 6484 for nationwide stockists. Traditional chintzes.
Designers' Guild, 267/271 & 277 King's Road, London SW3 5EN. Tel. 0171 243 7300. Contemporary wallpapers and fabrics in bold colours and designs.
Ian Mankin, 109 Regent's Park Road, London NW1 8UR. Tel. 0171 722 0997. Also 271 Wandsworth Bridge Road, London SW6 2TX. Tel. 0171 371 8825. Cotton checks, stripes and plains in Indian cotton. Good-value fabrics. Mail order available.
Jane Churchill, 151 Sloane Street, London SW1X 9BX. Tel. 0171 243 7300. Fabrics – prints, sheers and upholstery in traditional style but with a strong contemporary feel.

9BX. Tel. 0171 243 7300. Fabrics – prints, sheers and upholstery in traditional style but with a strong contemporary feel.
John Lewis. Tel. 0171 629 7711 for nearest branch.
John Wilman. Tel. 0800 581984 for nearest stockist.
Laura Ashley, 256 Regent Street, London W1. Tel. 0171 437 9760. For nearest branch Tel. 01628 622116.
Liberty, 210/220 Regent Street, London W1R 6AH. Tel. 0171 734 1234.
Manuel Canovas. Tel. 0171 225 2298.
Mrs Monro, 16 Motcomb Street, London SW1X 8LB. Tel. 0171 235 0326. English floral chintzes.
Osborne & Little, 304/308 King's Road, London SW3 5UH. Tel. 0171 352 1456. Tel. 0181 675 2255 for local stockists.
Sanderson, 112/120 Brompton Road, London SW3 1JJ. Tel. 0171 584 3344. Particularly known for the William Morris range of fabrics and wallpapers.
Timney Fowler, 388 King's Road, London SW3 5UZ. Tel. 0171 352 2263. Contemporary designs, mainly in black and white, based on classical architectural motifs.
Warner Fabrics. Tel. 01908 366900.

FLOORING, CARPETS & RUGS

Brahma Carpet Co, Kimberley House, 172 Billet Road, London E17 5DT. Mail-order traditional Eastern rugs. Write in for brochure.
Brintons Limited, PO Box 16, Exchange Street, Kidderminster, Worcestershire DY10 1AG. Tel. 01562 820000. Fax. 01562 748000 for a list of stockists. Finest quality carpets.
Campbell Marson, 573 King's Road, London SW6 2EB. Tel. 0171 371 5001. All types of hardwood flooring.
Crucial Trading, The Market Hall, Craven Arms, Shropshire SY7 9NY. Tel. 01588 67666. Phone for details of stockists. A very good selection of natural flooring, including sisal, coir and jute.
Fired Earth, Twyford Mill, Oxford Road, Adderbury, Oxfordshire OX17 3HP. Tel. 01295 812088. Natural jute, seagrass and coir floor covering.
Ian Walker, Odiham Gallery, 78 High Street, Odiham, Hampshire RG25 1LN. Tel. 01256 703415. Antique carpets, including rugs and kilims.
Natural Flooring Direct. Tel. 0171 252 3789 for mail order.
Roger Oates Design Associates, The Long Barn, Eastnor, Ledbury, Herefordshire. Tel. 01531 632718. Phone for stockists. Country-style rugs, carpets and jute.

PAINTS

Dulux. Tel. 01753 550555 for details of nearest stockist. Good range of Heritage colours to suit any period property.
Crown Paints, PO Box 37, Hollins Road, Darwen, Lancashire BB3 0BJ. Tel. 01254 704951.
Farrow & Ball, Uddens Estate, Wimborne, Dorset BH21 7NL. Tel. 01202 076141. Quality paints including the National Trust collection of 57 historical colours.
Fired Earth. Tel. 01295 812088. Range of eighteenth- and nineteenth-century colours developed in conjunction with the V & A Museum.
Helena Laidlaw, 15 Cresswell Gardens, London SW5. Tel. 0171 373 5673. Specialist painter. A wide range of sophisticated finishes. Will also paint furniture.
John Oliver, 33 Pembridge Road, London W11 3HG. Tel. 0171 727 3735. Hand-mixed quality paints, historical ranges.
Papers and Paints, 4 Park Walk, London SW10 0AD. Tel. 0171 352 8626. A range of historical paints as well as well-known ranges.

CURTAINS, SHUTTERS & BLINDS

American Shutters, 72 Station Road, London SW13 0LS. Tel. 0181 876 5905.
Calico Curtains. Tel. 01372 723846 for brochure. Plain and coloured calico blinds and curtains by mail.
Laura Ashley. Tel. 01628 770345 for nearest branch. See pages 37 and 42. Good range of made-to-order

ACCESSORIES

Aero, 96 Westbourne Grove, London W2 5RT. Tel. 0171 221 1950.

The Conran Shop, Michelin House, 81 Fulham Road, London SW3 6RD. Tel. 0171 589 7401. Excellent range of contemporary bedroom accessories including bedlinen, mirrors, etc.

The Holding Company, 243–245 King's Road, London SW3 5EL. Tel. 0171 352 1600. Storage systems, unusual ideas from America and Italy, modern accessories.

Habitat. Tel. 0645 334433 for nearest branch.

Ikea. Tel. 0181 451 5566 for nearest branch and catalogue. Flooring and storage systems.

Jerry's Home Store, 163/167 Fulham Road, London SW3 6SN. Tel. 0171 581 0909.

LIGHTING

Ann Lighting, 34a/b Kensington Church Street, London W8 4HA. Tel. 0171 937 5033. Fabulous range of traditional table lamps, bedside lights, reading lights. Good silk shades.

Bhs. Tel. 0171 262 3288 for branches. Excellent range of well-priced lamps, wall sconces, reading lights, both modern and traditional.

Christopher Wray, 600 King's Road, London SW6 2DX. Tel. 0171 736 8434. Period-style and contemporary light fittings.

John Cullen, 585 King's Road, London SW6 2EH. Tel. 0171 371 5400. Contemporary light fittings, and lighting consultants.

McCloud & Co, 269 Wandsworth Bridge Road, London SW6 2TX. Tel. 0171 371 5400. Contemporary and antiqued classical wall brackets, candle sconces.

Mr Light, 275 Fulham Road, London SW10. Tel. 0171 352 7525. Also at 279 King's Road, London SW3 5EW. Tel. 0171 352 8398. Vast range of modern lighting, wall lights, reading lights.

ASSOCIATIONS

National Asthma Campaign, Providence House, Providence Place, London N1 0NT. Tel. 0171 226 2260 (general enquiries), 0345 010203 (helpline).

The National Back Pain Association, The Old Office Block, 16 Elmtree Road, Teddington, Middlesex TW11 8ST. Send £2 for a copy of the members' magazine and leaflets on coping with back pain.

The National Bed Federation, 251 Brompton Road, London SW3 2EZ. Tel. 0171 589 4888

USA

ABC Carpet and Home, 888 Broadway, New York, NY 10003. Tel. 212 473 300. Floor coverings.

Benjamin Moore, 2501 West North Avenue, Melrose Park, IL 60160. Tel. 800 826 2623. Paints.

Bombay Company, PO Box 161009, Fort Worth, TX 76161. Tel. 800 829 7759. Furniture: traditional.

Brunschwig and Fills, 979 Third Avenue, New York, NY 10022. Tel. 212 838 7878. Wallpapers and fabrics.

The Company Store, 500 Company Store Road, LaCrosse, WI 54601. Tel. 800 323 8000. Bed linen.

Halo, 400 Busse Road, Elk Grove Village, IL 60007. Tel. 708 956 8400. Lighting.

Hold Everything, PO Box 7807, San Francisco, CA 94120 7807. Tel. 800 421 2264. Accessories.

IKEA, 1100 Broadway Mall, Hicksville, NY 11801. Tel. 516 681 4532. Furniture: contemporary.

Karastan, Box 130, Eden, NC 27288. Tel. 919 665 4000. Floor coverings.

Pier I Imports, PO Box 961020, Fort Worth, TX 76161-0020. Tel. 800 447 4371. Furniture: ethnic.

Pottery Barn, 100 North Point Street, San Francisco, CA 94109. Tel. 800 922 5507. Furniture/Accessories.

Room & Board, 4800 Olson Memorial Hwy, Minneapolis, MN 55422. Tel. 800 486 6554. Steel beds.

Sears, 3333 Beverly Road, Hoffman Estate, IL 60179. Tel. 800 499 9119. Paints.

Waverly, 79 Madison Avenue, New York, NY 10016. Tel. 800 423 5881. Wallpaper and fabrics.